Alfred's Premier Piano Course

Dennis Alexander • Gayle Kowalchyk • E. L. Lancaster • Victoria McArthur • Martha Mier

Alfred's *Premier Piano Course* Performance Book 2B includes motivational music in a variety of styles, reinforcing concepts introduced in the Lesson Book 2B. Duet accompaniments further encourage stylistic performances.

The pieces in this book correlate page by page with the materials in Lesson Book 2B. They should be assigned according to the instructions in the upper right corner of each page of this book. They also may be assigned as review material at any time after the student has passed the designated Lesson Book page.

A compact disc recording is included with this book. It can serve as a *performance* model or as a *practice* companion. See information about the CD on page 32. A General MIDI disk (23263) is available separately.

Performance skills and musical understanding are enhanced through *Premier Performer* suggestions. Students will enjoy performing these pieces for family and friends in a formal recital or on special occasions. See the List of Compositions on page 32.

Edited by Morton Manus

Cover Design by Ted Engelbart
Interior Design by Tom Gerou
Illustrations by Jimmy Holder
Music Engraving by Linda Lusk

ISBN-10: 0-7390-4140-1
ISBN-13: 978-0-7390-4140-6

Use with Alfred's Premier Piano Course, Lesson Book 2B, pages 4–5

Freight Train Boogie

CD 1/2   GM 1

Section A

Allegro

7

13

19

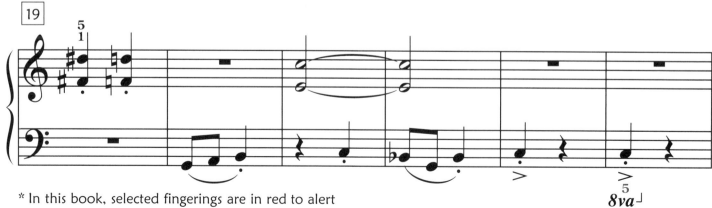

* In this book, selected fingerings are in red to alert
   the student to finger crossings or hand moves.

4

Treasure Island

CD 3/4   GM 2

Boldly, with spirit
The Captain

mf With a yo, heave ho! Raise the sails and go. There is treas-ure I must

find. Mark it on the map, is-land hab - i - tat, when we dig it up, it's

Slower
The Sailor

mine! Trim the sails, then swab the deck, that's my fate. For a sail-or, that's all there

be.   Keep-ing watch at night, what a plight,   up too late! Still, the   sail-or's life is for

Boldly, with spirit
The Captain

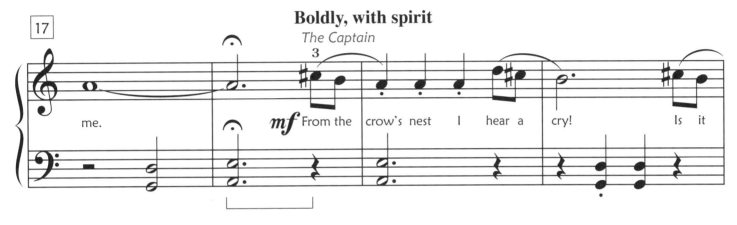

me.   *mf* From the crow's nest I hear a   cry!   Is it

land that he doth spy?   Drop the an - chor, mates, do not hes - i - tate. With a
mp   *mf rit.*   *f*
a tempo

yo, heave ho! Take the oars and row   to the   is-land with treas-ure that's mine!

Premier Performer — *Make a distinct change of tempo in measures 9 and 18 to convey the story.*

Lesson Book: pages 8–9

Louis Köhler (1820–1886) was a German conductor, teacher and critic. He composed over 300 works, most of which were piano etudes written for his own students.

Etude*

Louis Köhler
Op. 190, No. 31
Adapted by Alexander/Mier

Premier Performer — *Listen to play all RH eighth notes evenly.*

* *Etude* is the French word for "study." An etude is a short piece written to develop a specific technique. This etude works on developing an even, legato sound when playing five-finger patterns.

Duet: Student plays one octave higher.

Alexander/Mier

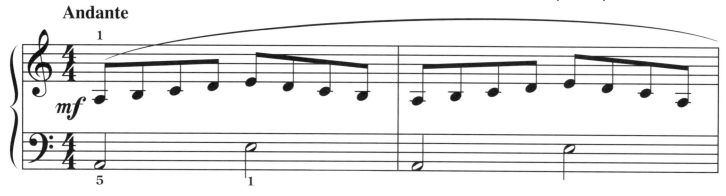

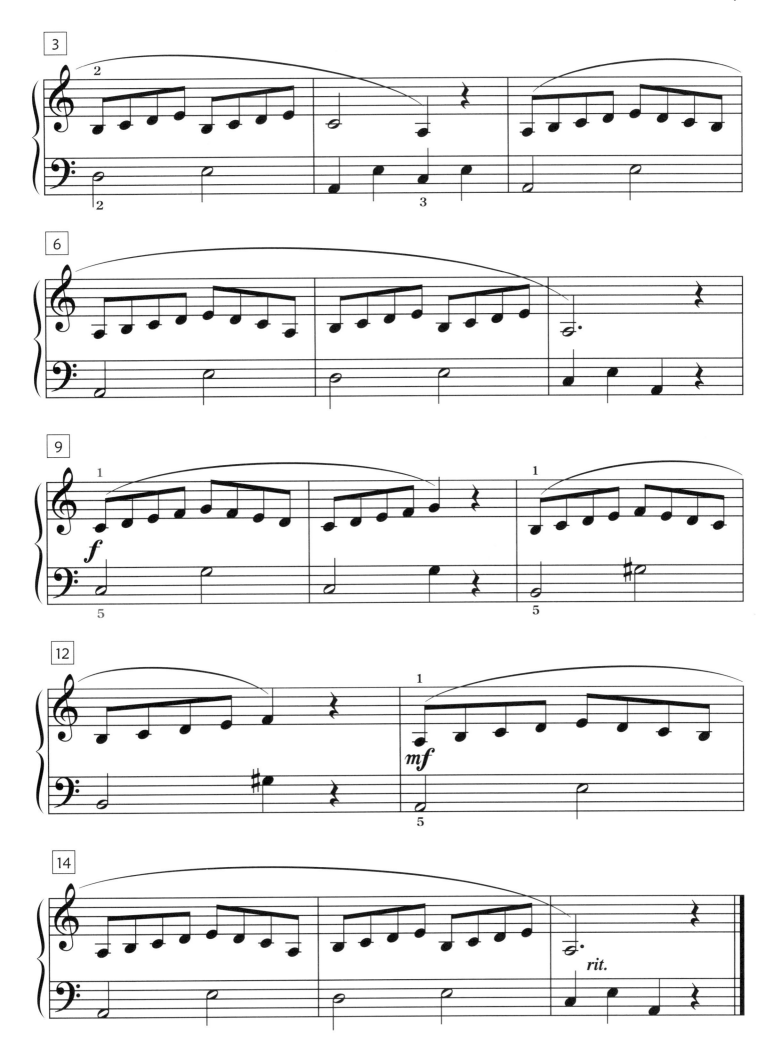

Lesson Book: page 10

Ode to Beethoven

CD 7/8   GM 4

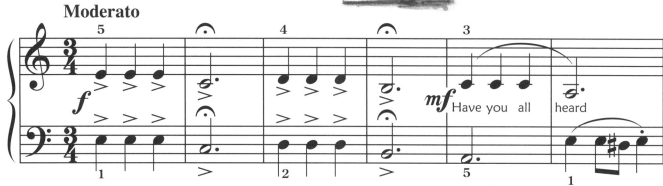

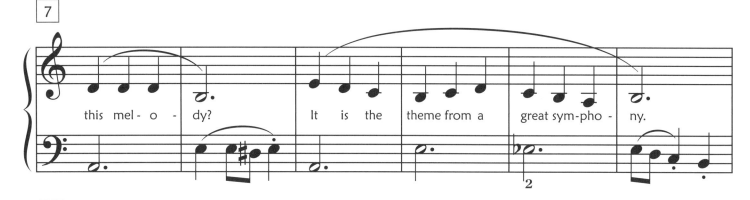

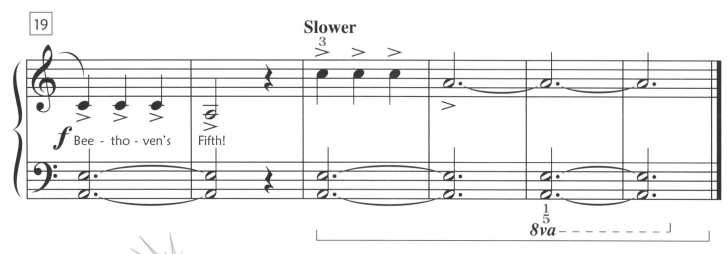

Premier Performer   *Play this piece with confidence and strong accents.*

Whirlwind

CD 9/10 GM 5

Moderately fast

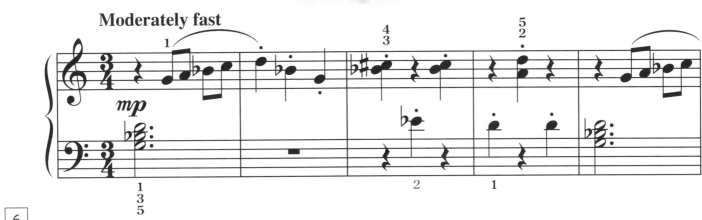

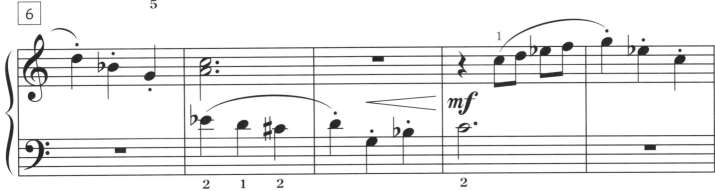

Premier Performer

Carefully observe all dynamics, slurs, staccatos and accents to create an exciting performance.

Evening Song

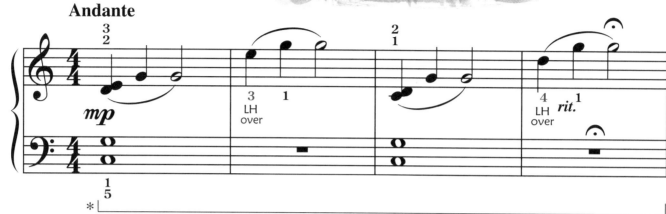

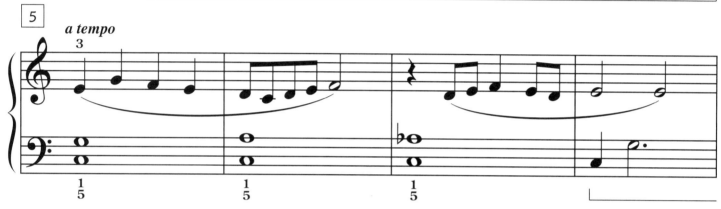

Duet: Student plays one octave higher.

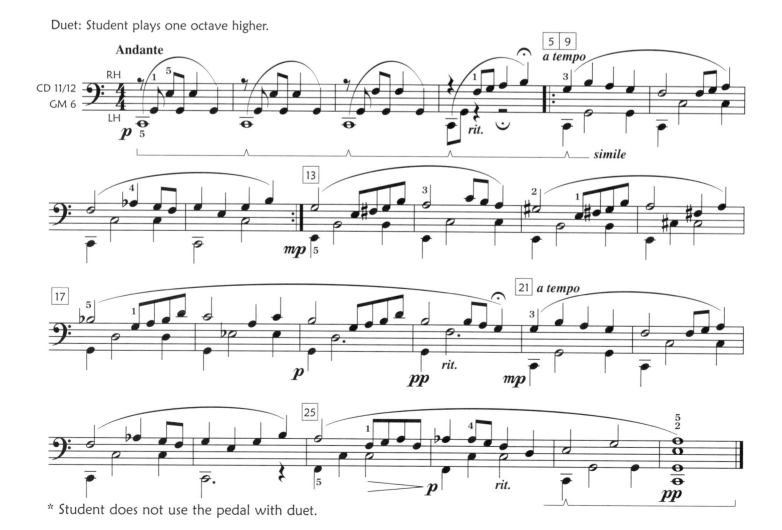

* Student does not use the pedal with duet.

Lesson Book: pages 16–17

Flamenco Dancers*

CD 13/14   GM 7

Moderately fast

* *Flamenco* is a colorful, rhythmic dance from Spain.

** Keep the quarter note beat steady between the 4/4 and 3/4 time signatures.

Seventh in Line

CD 15/16   GM 8

Moderato

I've got noth-ing that's mine. I'm sev-enth in

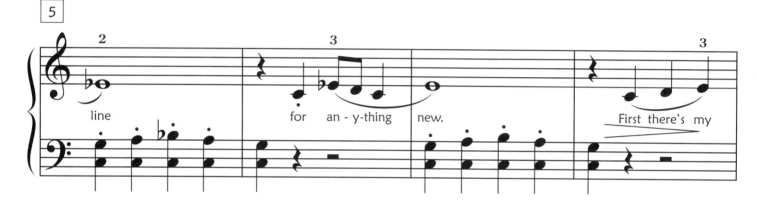

line for an-y-thing new. First there's my

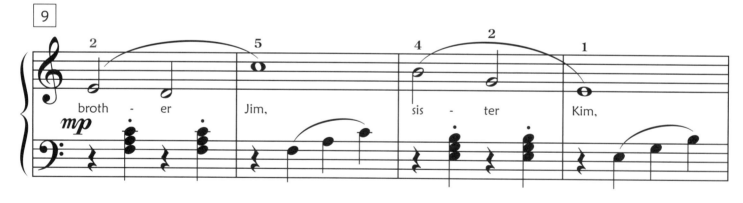

broth - er Jim, sis - ter Kim,

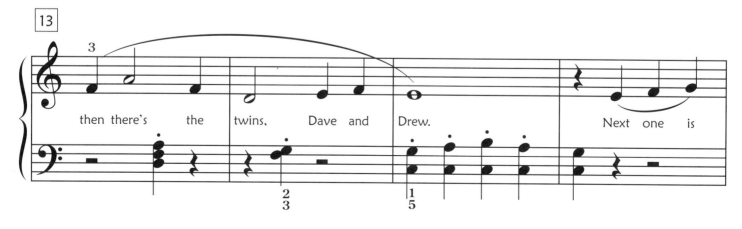

then there's the twins, Dave and Drew. Next one is

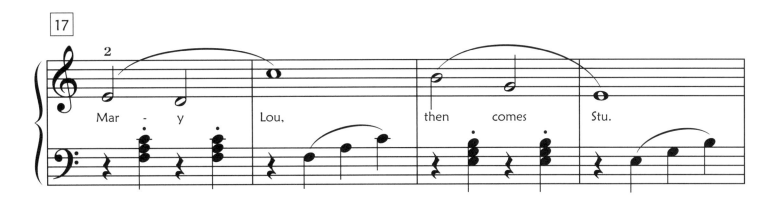

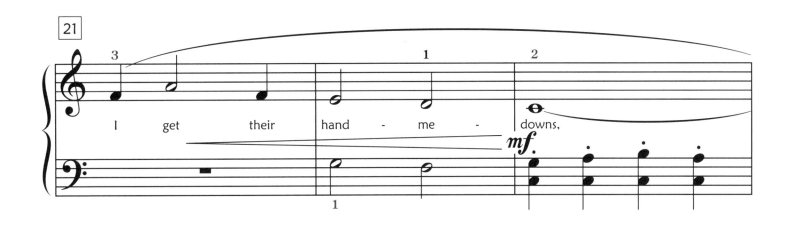

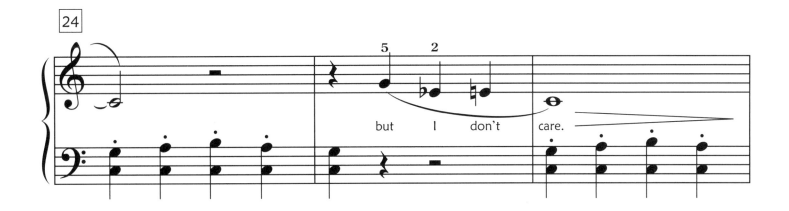

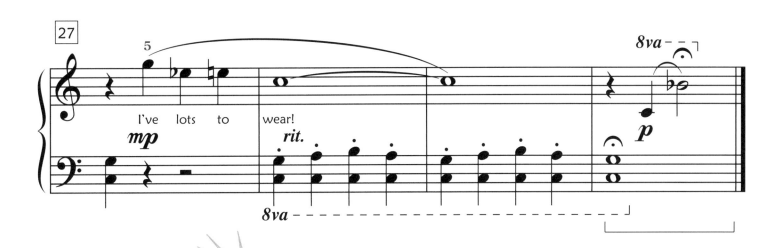

Premier Performer   *Keep the LH softer than the RH throughout.*

Lesson Book: page 23

Purple Twilight

CD 17/18   GM 9

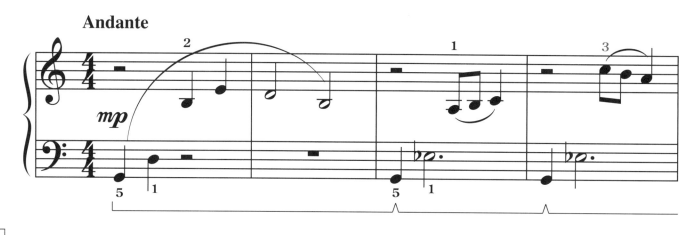

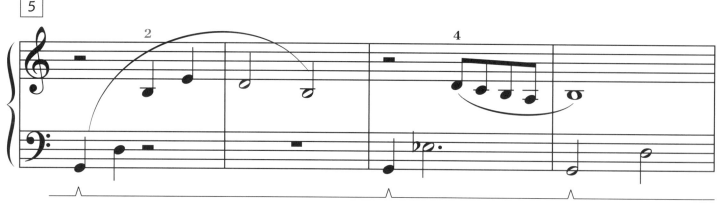

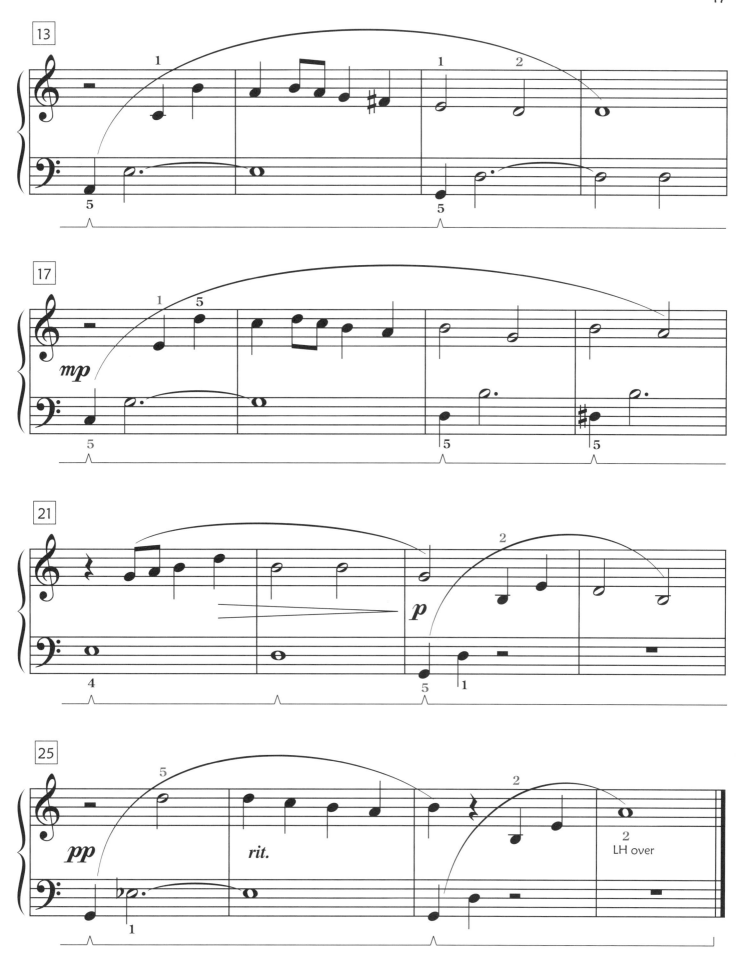

Premier Performer *Play with a gentle, legato touch throughout* Purple Twilight.

Chinese New Year

CD 19/20   GM 10

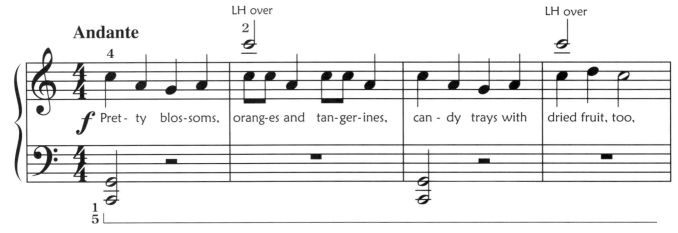

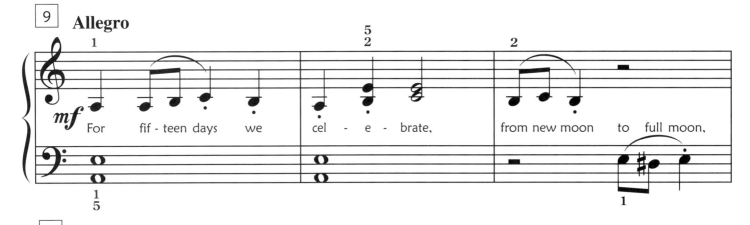

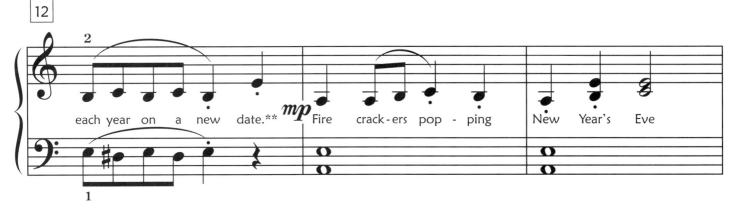

* These items are found in Chinese homes during New Year's celebrations.

** The Chinese calendar is based on movements of both the sun and moon.
On the solar calendar, Chinese New Year falls on a different date each year.

Premier Performer *Carefully observe all tempo changes.*

Lesson Book: pages 28–29

Ludvig Schytte (1848–1909) was born in Denmark. He first worked as a pharmacist and didn't begin to study music seriously until the age of 22. Among his teachers was the famous Hungarian composer, Franz Liszt. Schytte later taught at music conservatories in Vienna, Austria, and Bonn, Germany.

Short Story

Ludvig Schytte
Op. 108, No. 13

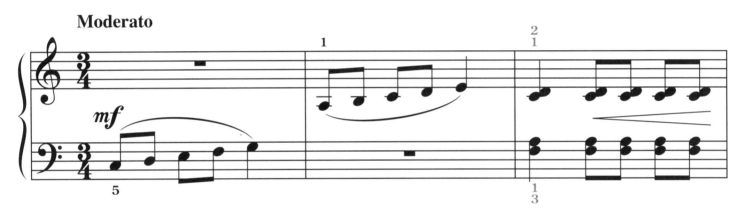

Alexander/Mier

Premier Performer

Play all the 5-finger patterns in Short Story with firm, strong fingers.

A Cool Waltz

CD 23/24   GM 12

Moderate waltz tempo

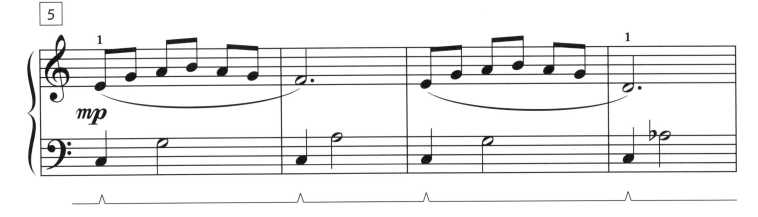

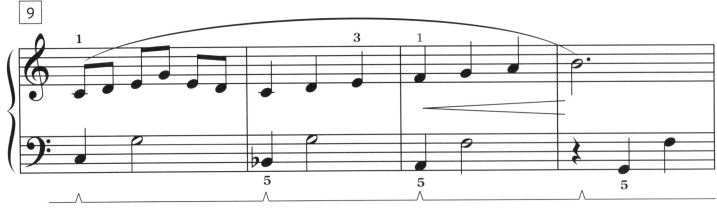

Premier Performer *Play with a relaxed feeling of three beats per measure—no pauses at the bar lines!*

Regal Dance

CD 25/26   GM 13

Section A

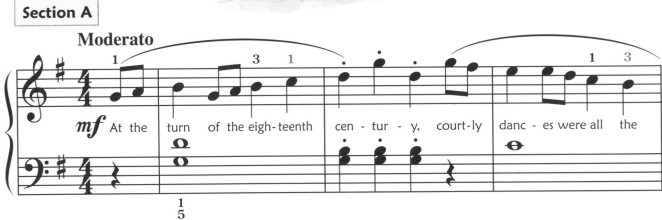

mf At the turn of the eigh-teenth cen-tur-y, court-ly danc-es were all the

rage. In the pal-ace of French king, Lou-is the Four-teenth, danc-ing

Section B

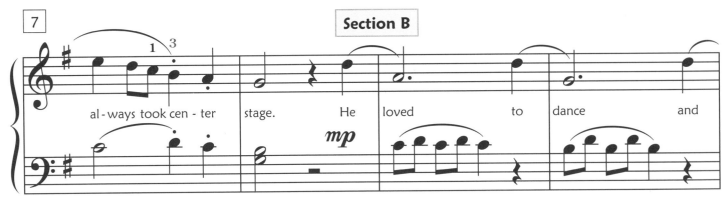

al-ways took cen-ter stage. He loved to dance and

gath-ered his no-bles at ev-'ry chance. They vied for roles. To

Section A

15

dance with the King was their goal. They spent ho - urs with danc - ing

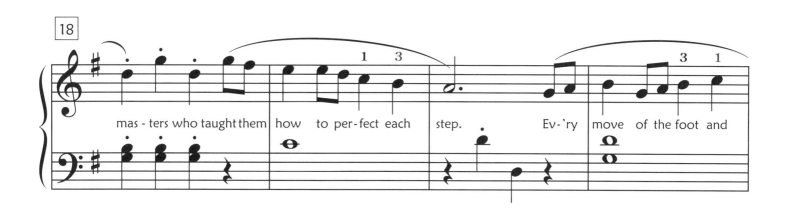

18

mas - ters who taught them how to per-fect each step. Ev-'ry move of the foot and

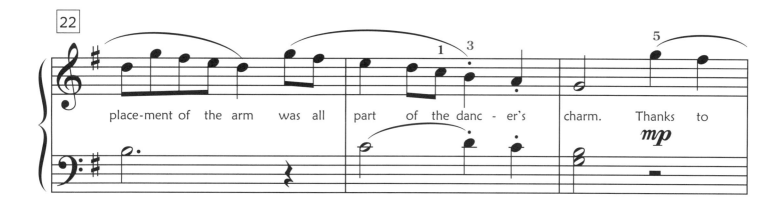

22

place-ment of the arm was all part of the danc - er's charm. Thanks to *mp*

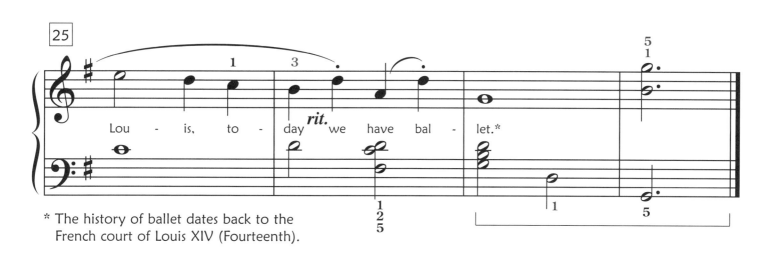

25

Lou - is, to - *rit.* day we have bal - let.*

* The history of ballet dates back to the
French court of Louis XIV (Fourteenth).

Premier Performer *Listen for a smooth legato sound when RH 1 passes under, or RH 3 crosses over.*

Banjo Tune

American Folk Song

Scrapbook Pages

CD 29/30   GM 15

Andante

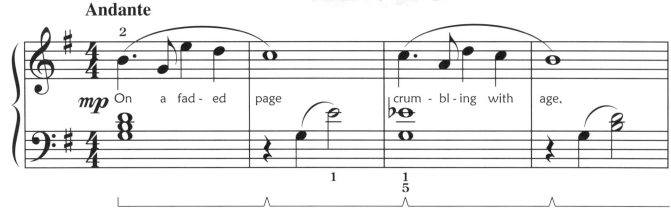

mp On a fad-ed page   crum-bl-ing with age,

5

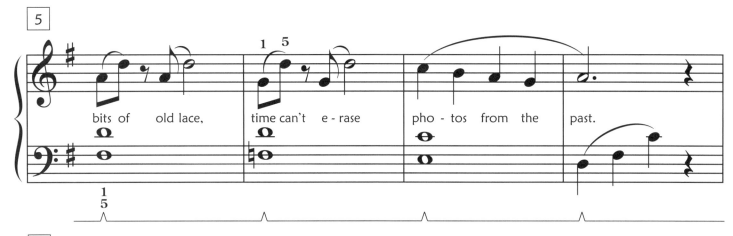

bits of old lace,   time can't e-rase   pho-tos from the past.

9

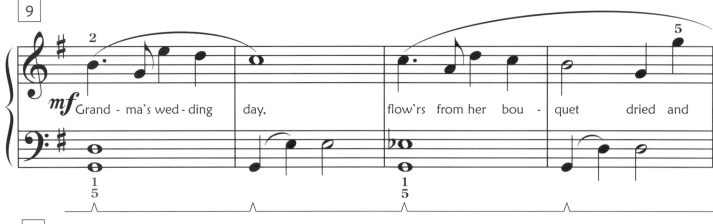

mf Grand-ma's wed-ding day,   flow'rs from her bou-quet dried and

13

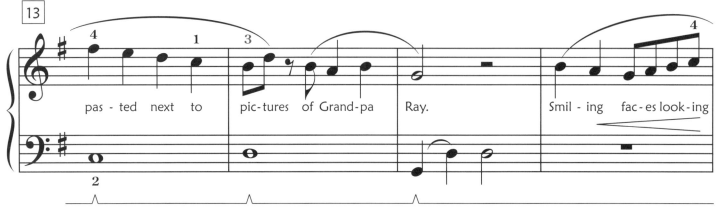

pas-ted next to   pic-tures of Grand-pa Ray.   Smil-ing fac-es look-ing

Listen for perfect balance between the melody and the accompaniment. Bring out the LH in measures 17–23.

Lesson Book: pages 46–47

Lemon Drop Rag

CD 31/32   GM 16

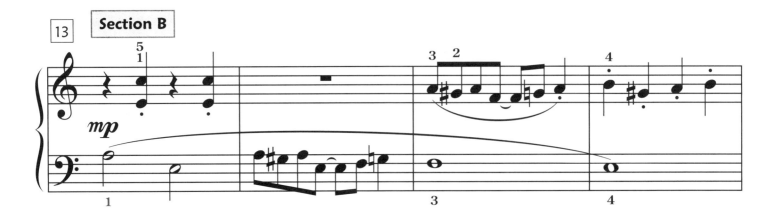

Section A

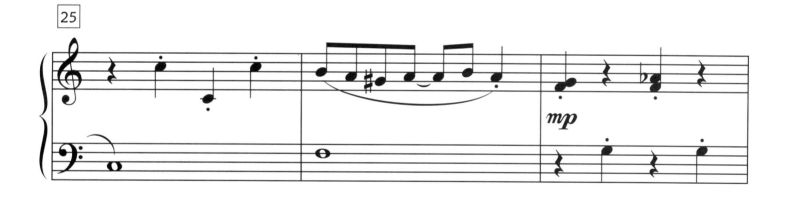

Premier Performer *Keep the tempo steady and relaxed.*

List of Compositions

Note: *Each selection on the CD is performed twice. The first track number is a performance tempo. The second track number is a slower practice tempo.*

The publisher hereby grants the purchaser of this book permission to download the enclosed CD to an MP3 or digital player (such as an Apple iPod®) for personal practice and performance.

CD Performances by Scott Price